The Airbus A380

A Tribute and Personal Memoir

Surendra C. Ratwatte

Copyright © Surendra Ratwatte 2020

2

FOREWORD

The Airbus A380 is one of the greatest feats of aerospace design and engineering the world has witnessed. That a machine of this size is capable of flight is itself amazing. That it can be mass-produced to allow passengers to travel with levels of safety and comfort that are taken for granted only a little more than 100 years since humans first mastered powered flight, is all but miraculous.

Airbus reinvented the wide-body jet with the A300, which was the first large twin-engine airliner built. This, and the subsequent success of the A320 single-aisle family, spurred the consortium to produce a complete suite of aircraft, with a commonality of design and technology, in order to compete effectively with Boeing, which had been the dominant manufacturer for several decades.

Airbus correctly forecast that 'ultra-long-range' (ULR) routes were an untapped market opportunity, and accordingly designed the four-engine A340 wide-body family. However, in doing so, Airbus committed the fundamental error of not anticipating that the increasing reliability and power of new-generation ducted turbofan engines would make long-range twinjets the preferred choice of airline customers.

While the A340-500 and -600 models were capable of unrestricted over-water flying, the unparalleled reliability of the large, improved engines powering Boeing's 777 made long over-water sectors possible for 'twins' as well. The cost savings of maintaining two engines (as opposed to four) meant that the A340 family was no longer an economic proposition.

The same reality has been the greatest hurdle to the A380's success. Market fragmentation and, at the time of writing, a pandemic that has effectively brought air travel to a standstill have sounded the death knell of Airbus's giant flagship.

This publication is one pilot's tribute to a wonderful example of man's aero-engineering ingenuity.

Suren Ratwatte
Melbourne, Australia.
August 2020.

4

Table of Contents

CHAPTER 1 — 7

LEARNING TO FLY THE AIRBUS A380 — 7

CHAPTER 2 — 14

FLYING THE A380 SIMULATOR — 14

CHAPTER 3 — 21

TOULOUSE, FRANCE –HOME OF AIRBUS — 21

CHAPTER 4 — 31

FIRST OPERATIONAL FLIGHT — 31
FLIGHT PREPARATION — 31
AT THE AIRPORT — 32
PRE-FLIGHT — 33
DEPARTURE — 34
BEGINNINGS OF TROUBLE — 35
THE DIFFICULT DECISION TO DIVERT — 36
THE DIVERSION — 37
APPROACH AND LANDING — 40
ON GROUND — 41
OVERWEIGHT LANDING — 42
MUNICH TO NEW YORK — 44

CHAPTER 5 — 47

A380 IN SERVICE-ONE YEAR AND COUNTING — 47
PUSHBACK AND ENGINE START — 50
DEPARTURE — 50
TOP OF CLIMB AND CRUISE — 51
DESCENT AND APPROACH — 54
LANDING AND PARKING — 55
SUMMARY OF PERFORMANCE — 56

CHAPTER 6 — 59

WHO KILLED THE AIRBUS A380? — 59
WHAT HAPPENED? — 59
MORE COMPLICATED THAN THEY THOUGHT — 61
ENTRY INTO SERVICE — 61
ONLY ONE LOVER — 62
A NICHE MARKETS — 63
WHAT IS THE FUTURE OF THE A380? — 63
AN EXERCISE IN HUBRIS — 64

CHAPTER 7 — 65

THE DEMISE OF THE 'UBER PLANE' — 65
WHY WOULD AN AIRLINE CHOOSE THE A380? — 65

THE FALLOUT FROM THE PANDEMIC 66
EMIRATES ARE THE OUTLIER 67
WHAT IS THE COST OF A PERMANENT GROUNDING? 68

CHAPTER 8 70

ROGER BÉTEILLE – THE MAN WHO REINVENTED THE COMMERCIAL AIRLINER **70**

Chapter 1

Learning to Fly the Airbus A380

(This chapter was first published in Airways *magazine, December 2008, under the pen name 'A Double-Decker Bus Driver'.)*

On the A380 training course, the first surprise is the absence of manuals. Usually, before the start date of a new-type course, participating pilots receive a polite message asking them to collect all the relevant manuals from the publications office. A reminder to bring a duffel bag to hold the many heavy books usually accompanies this.

Most of us, on the conversion course I most recently attended, are now too old to lug the books back home, so the smart guys bring their sons' cricket bags, the type with wheels at the bottom. This alleviates the load on our aging back muscles!

But the A380 is an airplane of the 21st century, so all we received were two DVDs. One has all the aircraft manuals on it, the other containing the ground course and study material. A bonus is that there will be no need for endlessly revised paper documentation, a chore that has driven many a pilot to the edge of despair.

Computers are provided in the training centre, of course, but everyone is required to have their own laptops. However, Macintosh users are incensed because the material will run only on Windows XP or higher. Insult added to injury.

The first day of the course is more like a veterans' reunion than anything else. All the captains are Emirates old-timers, friends who have known each other for 20 years or more, but other than on the occasional layover or at parties, have lost touch over the years. It is nice to catch up and compare stories and expectations. The co-pilots too are very close, being mostly from the same batch that joined the airline as cadets.

The first course with instructors – author is seated third from left

After a short introduction to the philosophy of the electronic manuals and the ground course, we are left to launch the application on our computers and start learning. The first thing we learnt was all the acronyms. Airbus is renowned for its fondness for such abbreviations, but on the A380 the array is mind-boggling. The manuals must seemingly be written in a suburb of Toulouse called 'Ville d'Acronyme'! Every item and system appears to have its own acronym and becoming familiar with them is going to take some time.

The next shock to the system is the numbers. This is a very big machine. Maximum gross take-off weight (MGTOW) is 569,000kg (1,254,430lb) with a maximum landing weight (MLW) of 391,000kg (862,000lb), and maximum zero fuel weight (MZFW) of 366,000kg (806,890lb). This will allow a maximum payload of around 66,000kg (145,500lb) to be carried for about 12 hours. The length of the aircraft is 72.7m (238.5ft)—albeit not the longest for an airliner—and its wingspan is 79.7 m (261.5ft), which is very large. Taxiing this beast at some airports promises to be an interesting chore.

Once we move into the 'guts' of the course, though, the sheer complexity of the A380 becomes evident. It is the logical extension of the trend that Airbus began with the then-revolutionary A320 in 1988. The basic philosophies of the original advanced flight control system, fly-by-wire (FBW) controls, side-stick controllers, etc, are still evident. But they have all been refined and carried to their logical conclusions.

Airbus has also unveiled its first electronic checklist. The ECAM (Electronic Centralised Aircraft Monitoring) that handled major failures still exists, but is now coupled to an electronic checklist that in turn is part of the Flight Warning Computer (FWC). All checklists—normal and abnormal—are run through the ECAM. Paper checklists have been effectively eliminated as well, with the dreaded QRH (Quick Reference Handbook—that was typically anything but) now running to only three pages: the Smoke and Emergency Evacuation checklists.

Even the ubiquitous laptop computers, which replaced the myriad charts and graphs used to calculate aircraft performance, are no more. Each pilot has a terminal with a keyboard on the table—an Airbus invention that Boeing pilots scoff at—which directly accesses the OIS (Onboard Information System) and allows calculation of take-off and landing performance, as well as accessing all the aircraft documents including an electronic aircraft technical log book.

The OIS screen also doubles as the display for the electronic charts. That's right—the days of injuring your back while lifting a heavy LIDO (or Jeppesen) manual from the chart bag are gone. Now the charts are electronic and appear on-demand on the screen. What is more, the charts can be resized, allowing the aging pilots among us to see the information without having to fish out reading glasses.

Indeed, the display screens for all this information rival a video arcade. In addition to the OIS display, which sits behind the side-stick controls, each pilot has three large rectangular LCD (liquid crystal display) screens that show enhanced versions of the PFD (Primary Flight Display), ND (Navigation Display), and FMS (Flight Management System). Two more LCDs are placed between the pilots, and these contain the ECAM display as well as the SD (System Display). All these screens are identical and interchangeable, allowing the pilots to display information on any one of them should a screen failure occur. The rectangular (as distinct from square) shape of the screens has allowed the manufacturer to squeeze in a lot more data on the same display. For example, the PFD—in addition to the now traditional attitude, airspeed, and altitude indicators, plus VSI (vertical speed indicator) and FMA (flight mode annunciator)—also displays flight control information and critical memo messages on the bottom of the screen.

No need to scan the centre panel for your flap setting, speed brake extension, etc. They are now right there in front of the pilot. The ND is particularly interesting, as the bottom of the screen displays a vertical display of the weather detected by the radar. So, while the conventional ND shows a plan view of the storms ahead, the bottom of the screen shows the same weather system, but from the side. In addition, this view can be skewed to left or right, allowing the pilots to pick their way through a line of storms. Equally clever is the function of the conventional ND that decides whether a storm ahead is below the aircraft, in which case it is shown crosshatched—a 'don't bother' hint to the crew.

All this magic is because Airbus has effectively reinvented the weather radar system, with the displays and information as separate entities. The radar antennae generate a three-dimensional view of what is 'seen', which is then stored in the database. This allows both lateral and vertical displays to be generated on the pilots' screens. Personally, I would like a hologram displaying the weather to appear in front of me so I can see exactly what is out there. Perhaps the next Airbus (A390) will have such a system!

In a further enhancement meant to ease flight crew workload in weather situations, it is possible now to define a waypoint using the trackball on the ND itself. No more incomprehensible waypoint, track and distance combinations needed. Just look at the weather depicted on the ND, pick a clear path, click the button, and *voila!* a new waypoint is created. These are automatically added to the flight plan, so navigation around a squall line, even at night, will be a lot less stressful. It is obvious to us that what until now was a chore, could even become a pleasure.

Even the standby instruments are small LCDs, capable of more functions and displays than a Casio watch. However, the magnetic compass is still on the main pillar, in all its analogue glory. This is a remarkable testament to both the simple functionality of the instrument and the aviation regulators' reluctance to fully embrace all the technology. It is probably the only instrument that a pre-Sixties aviator would recognize, and there is no conceivable failure that would cause the pilots to rely on it—but there it is.

Another first, at least for airliners, is the inclusion of a FMS Landing System (FLS) as a standard fit. This truly innovative technology, which has been on top-end business jets for some time, essentially removes the need for flying a non-precision approach (NPA). The very nature of NPAs—no glideslope information, the need for the use of vertically selected modes, etc—inherently led to many an unstable approach and landing accidents. But the FLS practically eliminates this danger. By using a reference approach—usually a VOR (Very High Frequency Omnidirectional Radio Range)-based one and the known runway information—the FMS database creates a 'virtual' ILS (instrument landing system)-type approach, using the runway as an 'anchor point'. This is presented to the pilot in exactly the same way as an ILS, the only differences being the magenta 'double diamond' course deviation indicators, and the notation of the anchor point (rather than the ILS identification) on the PFD. Once the approach is selected, and checked for accuracy against the published chart on which it is based, the pilot flies it exactly the same as an ILS approach. Because glideslope information is displayed, potential errors caused by having to manually crosscheck the descent path are eliminated. In the long list of improvements on the A380, the FLS function will rate very highly amongst all pilots fortunate enough to fly this magnificent airplane.

But Airbus has gone even further, with some systems having also been 're-invented' in their entirety—in particular, the hydraulic system. Since flight controls became large enough to need more than pilots' muscular strength to activate, hydraulic failures have been the bugbear of aircraft designers (remember Captain Al Haynes and the United DC-10 incident at Sioux City, Iowa?). So, the A380, with control surfaces the size of barn doors, 22 wheels, and 5,000psi (350kg/cm^2) hydraulic systems to move it all, needed something special. Airbus engineers addressed the issue, and the aircraft has only two hydraulic systems—ostensibly.

However, the failure of both these systems is almost a non-event, and leads only to a master caution light (an amber warning rather than a red light warning of emergency). This is because of the invention that Airbus calls Electro-Hydrostatic Actuators (EHA) and Electrical Backup Hydraulic Actuators (EBHA). These are essentially independent systems, with their own reservoirs, that generate hydraulic power as and when required—especially for critical flight control surfaces. So even a complete, catastrophic failure that damages all the main systems and drains all the fluid, will leave pilots with the important flight controls still powered and able to extend the landing gear by gravity. While this may not seem like much to a layperson, it is a huge achievement, one that every pilot will admire. Someday, I must meet the team that designed this and buy them all a beer.

The associated flight control system has also been improved. It continues the Airbus philosophy of 'protections'. While this is not every pilot's cup of tea it does work very well. The system has been tweaked to make engine failures even more benign, and has a few tricks to prevent tail-strike and make the nose wheel touch down a little smoother. A little more improvement and, seemingly, pilots may not be required at all.

Undoubtedly the most complex system on the A380 is the fuel system. It comprises 11 tanks capable of holding over 323,500l (84,110USg), with 20 pumps to deliver fuel to the engines. This takes place in an elaborately choreographed process that not only ensures adequate fuel flow to each engine, but also maintains an optimum centre of gravity (CG) and alleviates wing-bending moments by transferring fuel between the tanks. The system is so complex that the ECAM has two pages devoted to its operation: the 'normal' display, and 'more' display that shows the system in all its mind-boggling complexity. This is one system that this old pilot hopes will work as advertised—understanding it is hard enough; troubleshooting it would be darned near impossible.

Almost as complex, though easier to grasp, is the landing gear. With the nose gear, two wing landing gears (four wheels per bogie), and two body landing gears (six wheels per bogie) there is certainly a lot of rubber on the road. Sixteen of the wheels have brakes, and in addition to the nose gear, the aft bogies on the body gear are steerable. All this enables the behemoth to turn on a dime—well almost, given its size.

It is not my intention here to bore readers with details of all the systems on this mighty machine. Suffice it to say that the engineering design team has incorporated all the lessons learned over a half-century of jetliner operations and tried hard to plug all the holes. This is a complete package, and one this humble pilot regards as a masterpiece. From the pilot's point of view, of course, the most important factor is how the airplane flies. That is first discovered in the simulator—our next step. ✈

Chapter 2

Flying the A380 simulator

(This first appeared in Airways *magazine, January 2009, under the same pen name as the previous chapter.)*

Puny is what most human pilots feel as they approach the simulator every six months, with their licenses and livelihoods at stake. But facing up to a simulator as part of a transition course is an entirely different thing. This is the chance to come to grips with an airplane that so far has existed only in the realms of theory and 'virtual reality'. Knowledge acquired so painfully via computer screens and books, is about to gain a third, tactile dimension—and become real.

The realism of modern simulators is quite astonishing. This writer's first encounter with a full-motion simulator was one mounted on railway tracks. It would lunge forward or back to simulate movement and then creep forward, at a rate calculated to be imperceptible, until it was back at the neutral position. The display of this machine was primitive too: only a night vision-type monochrome view through the front windows. Even this somewhat primitive machine needed considerable computing power, though, with roomfuls of cabinets and a coterie of acolytes devoted to its upkeep.

Today's six-axis simulators have visual displays that are quite astonishing in their accuracy, a degree of fidelity that is being constantly refined, and probably more computing power than NORAD (North American Aerospace Defence Command) had in its heyday. They have changed so much from the first of their ilk, and the experience offered is so close to an actual airplane, that pilots are allowed to do all their training in a simulator, with the first actual landing with passengers in the back, allowing the airlines massive cost savings in their training programs. But the price of these marvellous machines is also high. A simulator costs almost as much as a small passenger aircraft and requires enormous computing power, as well as enough electrical power to light up a small suburb. However, given the price of an aircraft and the jet fuel to power it, they are an amazing bargain.

A380 simulator in Dubai

Even the characteristic hiss and sigh of the hydraulic arms that held the 'cockpit' aloft and allowed those six axes of motion are no more. The very latest simulators are on electrically driven screw jacks that are almost totally silent, taking away another of this old aviator's memories.

But I digress. This piece is about learning to fly (or 'operate', in modern parlance) the Airbus A380. In the punishing world of airline finances, even a simulator, which costs a fraction of the price of an A380, is expensive.

A pilot's first encounter with the machine takes the form of a FTD (fixed training device), or systems mockup. This is much more prosaic than a simulator and consists of a collection of touch-sensitive LCD screens— any one of which would look really cool in my living room—that display all the panels that pilots will encounter in the airplane. All the switches can be 'moved' by touching the screen, and the computers ensure that the appropriate commands and changes are displayed on the other instruments and systems affected by a change. Every phase of flight is possible to emulate, and the principal use of the FTD is to ensure that pilots are familiar with placement of controls and indicators so that all normal procedures—and many abnormal ones—can be practiced to a reasonable degree of fidelity.

There is no visual display, but the FTD can be 'flown' by reference to the instruments. The engines can be started (there is even a whine through the speakers), flaps extended, thrust levers moved to the takeoff position, and the instruments show that the aircraft is moving. Once rotation speed (Vr) is reached, a tap on the side-stick and we are 'airborne'. The 'virtual' gear is retracted, flaps stowed on schedule, and off we go.

In a word, the FTD is boring. But it serves a useful purpose. The entire cockpit scans and checklist flows can be practiced over and over until they are second nature. This familiarity with the flight deck is one of the hardest phases of learning to fly a new aircraft. On the type you have flown for a time, the scans and flows are second nature. Most pilots can do the cockpit set-up and normal checklists while flirting with a flight attendant and drinking coffee. These are practically second nature once we have 'time on type', but on a new aircraft we feel like two-year-olds in a nuclear plant. Getting the basic knowledge and muscle memory stored is a vital part of a conversion; and the FTD, tedious as it is, plays a vital role in the training process.

Another important skill acquired in the FTD is the use of the FMS (Flight Management System). Airbus has a very different approach to that of the other manufacturer, and the FMS on the A380 is different again from the previous generation. For starters, the screen is much bigger, allowing much more data to be displayed. For those of us who have essentially grown up with the standard six-line FMS displays in most commercial applications, this is as transforming as your first encounter with a wide-screen computer. "Hey look, the track and distance are on the same page!" Quite a revelation in the nerdy world of airline pilots.

Finally—the real simulator. After many sessions in the FTD, becoming used to the 'new' (for Airbus) electronic checklists and all the other gizmos on the A380, we finally have a chance to taste the real thing— well, sort of. Fresh from a software upgrade to incorporate the flight data from the A380 demonstrator that has been travelling around the world, this marvel of modern science is about to provide our first full-flight simulator session.

One of the more annoying facets of simulators is that the displays and information they use to simulate real flight are not necessarily real-time and up-to-date. For example, when there is a new taxiway or radio aid at an airport, chances are that the simulator will not incorporate this for many months. Actually, updating the computer database and generating the required visuals is a time- and money-consuming process, necessarily constrained in this budget-conscious era. In order to take away this annoyance, Airbus Training has done something rather clever. They have 'invented' an entire airport. Enjoying the fictitious ICAO code of 'LFZZ', this is an airport that never changes. All its runways are large and long enough to accommodate the world's largest airliner, there is very little traffic, and the navies never change. The weather, of course, is at the whim of the simulator instructor, and LFZZ is capable of 'experiencing' snow and sleet on any given day of the month.

All training flights for this first part of the conversion course originate out of LFZZ. The layout of the airport is such that budding A380 pilots can operate on taxiways with no restriction despite the 80m (262.5ft) wingspan of the beast. Taxiing on more restrictive layouts will be something we are called on to do at most airports when flying the real aircraft of course, but for now it is not an issue. We can even practice doing a 180° turn on the taxiways, a manoeuvre this pilot sincerely hopes he will never have to perform in the actual airplane.

In fact, taxiing is going to be one of the major challenges on the double-decker. Its main wheels are 14.4m (47.3ft) apart, so keeping to the centreline of the taxiway becomes a vital task. The taxi cameras located on the top of the vertical stabilizer and on the fuselage beneath the airplane help the pilots to check the wheels' actual position. As a further aid, magenta indicators on the display denote the position of the main gears.

The simulator has a nifty little program that also places arrows on the visual display, showing the pilots where the aircraft's engines are located. This is essential because the tapering of the fuselage means that pilots are unable to see the wing tips, let alone the engines, from their seats. This is one of the instances when the wisdom of the ICAO

(International Civil Aviation Organization) Code F—for airport design (equivalent to FAA Group VI) with wide taxiways and extra spacing between them and the runways—comes into its own. Unfortunately there are only a handful of Code F airports in the world, ironically most of them in Asia and none due for A380 operations anytime soon.

Turning the A380 on the taxiway is something that takes getting used to. It is necessary to lead the turns a considerable amount, and this is where the cameras are essential. The body wheel steering (on the last pair of bogies of the six-wheel landing gear) works for the pilots in ensuring that turns are kept relatively tidy. It is fairly easy to make a 180° turn on a 60m (197ft) taxiway—at least in the simulator.

Again I digress. Now it's time to fly the simulator and accomplish a normal takeoff. Position the thrust levers to the takeoff 'gate'—a peculiarity of the non-moving thrust levers that are standard on Airbus FBW (fly-by-wire) aircraft—at a takeoff weight of 540t (1,190,500lb), well below the maximum of 569t (1,254,430lb), and the acceleration of the simulator is best described as stately.

After a not inconsiderable period, the auto call "Vee one" is heard, and soon after the PNF (pilot not flying) calls "Rotate." A smooth increase of pitch toward the target angle of 12.5° and we are airborne. This first simulator session is about normal manoeuvres and exploring the handling characteristics of the aircraft. It is a joy to fly—smooth and light at the controls but with a considerable amount of inertia. First impressions are all positive. The A380 is very responsive, needing only two fingers on the side-stick to manoeuvre, and extremely stable. Airbus philosophy is that the side-stick is simply another input device. It is used to adjust the attitude of the aircraft to the appropriate position. The automation and the auto-throttle do the rest. This being the first time, of course we all tend to 'hand fly' the simulator as much as we can. But it is so smooth and precise that we give up and engage the autopilot not very long into the session.

Given the degree of automation, calling every change on the FMA (Flight Mode Annunciator) is an Airbus requirement. This is because the FMA tells the pilots exactly what system is controlling every aspect of the flight. Some of the changes are quite subtle but nevertheless important, and calling out FMA changes is going to have to become second nature.

The next few days are full. We are put through the whole range of maneuvers that are required by the regulator to prepare us for the proficiency test. The flying is relatively easy, because the A380 is designed (or should I say 'programmed'?) to handle very much like the other Airbus FBW aircraft. If anything, it is more benign, probably because of refinements in the software and the massive inertia of the aircraft. Crosswind landings are fairly straightforward, the only trick being to de-crab in the flare. The maximum certified crosswind component was 30kt at the time of training, but this will probably be raised once in-service experience is gained (56kt was demonstrated during flight testing).

Operations with an engine failed are also benign, while the dreaded 'engine failure at V_1' is almost a non-event. The Airbus sideslip index is a great help in this case, assisting the pilot in gently applying the required amount of rudder (very little is needed) to form a pyramid on the indicator and assure coordinated flight with asymmetrical thrust. Throughout the maneuver, the simulator remains very stable and forgiving, a pleasure to fly.

This is the first Airbus type with a full electronic checklist. Previous aircraft had the ECAM (Electronic Centralized Aircraft Monitor), which required a bulky paper checklist to back it up, unlike the rival manufacturer's version. A mere five pages long, the A380's paper version caters only for a complete electrical failure, a statistically improbable event.

The electronic checklist (ECL) takes a little getting used to. It is complex and requires a considerable amount of 'head-down' time from the non-flying pilot. But it is also capable of dealing with every possible failure and, in the vast majority of cases, providing instant feedback on pilot actions. Those who have used Boeing's version tend to be a little grudging in their praise, but we all learn to operate it efficiently.

During normal operations, the real value of the ECL is apparent. Earlier, the request for a checklist meant the PM (pilot monitoring) had to locate the QRH (Quick Reference Handbook), possibly turn on a reading light and fumble for reading glasses, while reciting the checklist that was printed on a worn and sometimes torn piece of cardboard with an often opaque protective cover. Not anymore. A simple button pushes and, 'Hey presto!' the checklist menu appears on the center LCD, usually with the correct checklist highlighted. One more push and the checklist is displayed, with the completed items already in green.

Typically, only the 'challenge and response' items need to be manually verified to complete the checklist. Once this is verified by the PF (pilot flying), the display can be de-selected allowing the default information to be made visible. It is a very ergonomic and pilot-friendly piece of equipment that reduces workload considerably whilst also increasing safety.

As it turns out, the simulator program has no surprises for us, and our entire trainee group completes it without problems. The only areas we are unable to master are the use of the electronic charts, the OIS (Onboard Information System)—which has all the aircraft manuals, performance applications, navigation charts, and even an electronic logbook—because, unfortunately, the simulator does not fully support this application.

The next step is the biggest plum of all: a chance to fly the A380 around Europe for the IOE (initial operating experience) part of our training. Usually this takes place on a company aircraft on domestic routes, but because our first A380 is yet to be delivered, the initial group of pilots has to go to the home of Airbus—a treat to which we are all looking forward. ✈

Chapter 3

Toulouse, France –home of Airbus

Paris in the springtime is a wonderful place—or so the poets tell us. In this case, though, it was only Charles de Gaulle Airport, and Paris was not our final destination. But, no worries, we were headed to Airbus HQ at Toulouse in the southern part of France, nestled close to the Spanish border, by the Pyrenees mountain range.

Twenty-five years ago Toulouse was a small place, best known for its universities and 'old city', a walled enclave dating from medieval times. Toulouse-Blagnac International Airport itself has a long and distinguished history, having been in existence since 1928. The iconic French jetliner, the Sud-Aviation Caravelle, was built here, and so was the supersonic Anglo-French Concorde. Airbus Industry set up its administration and manufacturing headquarters at Toulouse in 1970, thus cementing the area's place in aviation folklore, whilst sparking massive growth.

After a rather jet-lagged sleep, we pitch up at the Airbus Training Centre, a large, straggling building that has obviously grown along with the company, for a briefing and collection of IDs and paperwork. A brief tour takes us past simulators for all Airbus types, and we meet some of the pilots who are being trained to fly them. This is followed by lunch at the Airbus staff canteen, a very 'French' eating place with a choice of salads, starters, four main courses, freshly made pizza, and a dessert selection that would rival that of any gourmet restaurant. Very enjoyable on a wet afternoon with nothing to do, especially because the canteen also liberally dispenses very drinkable vin *de table*. We return to our hotel intent on an early night and hoping for good weather the next morning.

Clear skies herald the next day, but it is chilly as we huddle on the pavement waiting for a taxi. In the early gloom we speed past streets still wet from the night's rain, our excitement increasing as we near the airport. After a short wait at the gate we are met by Nick, one of the Airbus test pilots, and off we go to the test flight hangar located in the Zone Aéronautique on the west side of the airfield.

We drive past rows of gleaming new airliners awaiting completion and delivery, mostly A320s but many wide bodies too, painted in the colors of airlines from all over the world. At the hangar, Nick leads the way to the briefing room. Unable to resist the temptation, we ignore the documentation and go to the windows to get our first look at the airplanes—and there they are: F-WWOW and F-WWDD (MSNs 001 and 004, respectively), two of the first four A380s built, looking resplendent in the early morning light.

A380 being readied for delivery at Toulouse

Tearing ourselves away from the window, we reluctantly turn to find two more people in the room, wryly observing our excitement. These are Michel Landrin, head of flight and cabin crew training, and Flight Engineer Pascal Verneau, who will fly with us today.

The next half-hour is spent going over the documents, weather, and flight plan. We are to fly to two regional airports close by so we can acquire the relevant flying time and landings required to complete our IOE. Sufficient fuel is carried to ensure that we take off close to MLW (maximum landing weight), thereby giving us an idea as to how the airplane would handle at typical approach speeds. The meteorological briefing shows fine weather all over France, which means that visibility is going to be excellent and conditions benign. The airports selected for the landings, Châteauroux-Déols in central France, and Chalon-Champforgeuil, to the east of Paris, are former military fields with long runways but little traffic.

With mounting excitement we walk out to the aircraft. Pascal, who is the custodian of this airplane (his 'handle', 'VNO,' is even painted on the nose wheel door, thus establishing his 'ownership') has already completed the walk-around inspection and ensured the aircraft is fit for flight.

A380 VNO with the author
Note the signatures of other pilots who have trained on the aircraft on the nose-wheel doors

The first impression as we approach F-WWDD on foot is the sheer size of the A380. Its bulk is amazing, and the passenger steps that reach the main deck door are barely halfway up the side of the fuselage. The 'inverted gull-wing' design manages to look light and fluid, an impression quickly contradicted by the thickness of the wings and the dramatic size of the engines. For example, the inboard engine is high enough for the head of a person of average height to be level with the bottom edge of the cowling. The outboards are as high as a Boeing 737's tail. And the width of the horizontal stabilizer equals the wingspan of a 737—the first jet type this aviator flew.

Up the steps and we arrive at a cavernous and practically bare interior with a huge cross-section. Immediately on the left is a narrow flight of steps leading to the flight deck door. On the right a much wider stairway leads to the upper-deck passenger cabin. There is no time to explore, though—into the flight deck and left seat, strap in, and begin the pre-flight. This stage is rushed, because time is of the essence and the object of the training mission is aircraft handling. The checklist and cockpit drills can be practiced in the simulator; what is important today is to become airborne. Our route is a standard one that Airbus uses for training, so it is available in the database. Airbus training pilots help out with the preparation, so in short order we are ready to push back and start the engines. The western (or Colomiers) side of the airport is quiet, with commercial flights using the Blagnac side and usually Runway 33R.

After a short taxi to 33L, we are cleared for takeoff. Taking a deep breath, I stand up the thrust levers, eliciting a rumble from the four Rolls-Royce Trent 900 engines, and the A380 starts to roll majestically down the runway. The takeoff run is short (I doubt that we will ever operate at this takeoff weight in airline service); then Michel announces "V_r" [rotation speed]; I ease back on the side-stick—and we are airborne.

So far, so good. I haven't embarrassed myself yet and it flies just like the simulator. The view out of the huge cockpit windows is superb. But I have to tear my eyes away and concentrate on flying the airplane. ATC (air traffic control) rattle out instructions to take us away from the terminal area, and then it becomes quiet as we level off and I engage the autopilot. Châteauroux is about 35 minutes' flying time away, enough to get the feel of the A380—I hope.

"You are comfortable?" Michel asks from the right seat, as Pascal helpfully produces a flask of coffee and a tray full of delectable-looking French pastries. "This is training today—you can play as much as you like."

A view of the instruments – note the LFBO airport char to the right.

That is invitation enough, and after a quick slug of caffeine and a bite of croissant I ask what I am permitted to do with the aircraft.

"Anything you like," was the helpful reply.

"Steep turns?" I ask. A nod in affirmation.

"VLS?" [lowest selectable airspeed] ('I'm pushing it now,' I think to myself.)

"OK, if you have not seen this, it is good—go all the way to 'alpha-floor'."

(To avoid flying at low speed with low thrust, the Airbus FBW types have a safety feature known as alpha-floor, or ∝-floor. This function automatically applies TOGA (Takeoff Go Around) thrust when the AoA

25

(angle of attack) exceeds the ∝-floor threshold, located between the AoA that Airbus calls ∝-prot—where the speed protection threshold begins—and ∝-max, the maximum AoA, very close to stall speed.)

I look across at him incredulously—this is better than being a kid let loose in a candy store!

Making sure that everybody is secured and that ATC is aware that we need a block of airspace, we make a couple of gentle turns to ensure that F-WWDD is all alone in this little patch of French sky. I disconnect the autopilot, turn on the flightpath vector—a handy Airbus tool that displays real-time flightpath information on the PFD (Primary Flight Director)—and gently roll the aircraft into a bank. As the turn steepens, at 45° the flight director is automatically removed. The view out of the windows is quite astonishing now; the horizon is at an angle I have never seen on a large aircraft. It becomes more radical as I approach 60° of bank and the pressure needed on the side-stick, both turn input and back pressure to remain in level flight, becomes considerable. I am using my whole hand (no more two-finger stuff) and most of my strength to achieve this. Somewhere around 67° of bank, I hit the 'stop'; the built-in protection will not allow the bank angle to increase any farther. But reaching this limit was not easy, and it is unlikely to be wilfully achieved under any conceivable situation. I am concentrating too hard to really enjoy the view, but manage a sneak peek—pretty impressive to see the ground out of the side window at that angle!

Once back in level flight I disconnect the auto-thrust, reduce thrust to idle and start to gently pull back on the stick to maintain level flight. The speed decays slowly as the big airplane pitches up. Speed continues to decrease, and at ∝-prot I release the side-stick and the aircraft maintains that speed in slight descent. This is slower than approach speed and is what would happen if the aircraft becomes 'low and slow' on approach. To reach ∝-max, which is still above the stall speed, it would be necessary to maintain full back-pressure on the stick—not as easy as it sounds, and very unlikely at low altitude. At this speed the protections would come into play, as the auto thrust would apply full TOGA thrust in order to protect the flightpath and prevent an uncontrolled descent into the ground.

In this case, I allow the airplane to recover by repositioning the thrust levers to the cruise detent, reducing the pitch angle and re-engaging the autopilot and auto-thrust. Speed recovers; we regain our cleared altitude, and continue on our way. The stability and benign handling of the A380, even at this extreme end of the envelope, are very encouraging.

The interior of MSN 004/F-WWDD is set up for flight-testing. Occupying much of the lower deck is a series of tanks and pipes comprising a water ballast and CG (centre of gravity) control system. During an extended flight, the CG of the aircraft changes as fuel is transferred between the trim tank (located in the horizontal stabilizer) and the main tanks. On the test airplane, by pumping water between the various tanks it is possible to replicate this change in CG without the need to fly for long periods of time.

The author and course mate Moataz Al Swaini at the monitoring station

Also on the lower deck are data control and monitoring stations. These record a variety of flight parameters for analysis in the laboratory. A series of monitors is used to display real-time flight information, the flight deck instruments, or a variety of other data. The control unit can also generate and print out data for a specific flight, including exact measurements of the g-load on touchdown, the distance from the threshold that touchdown took place, the exact displacement from centreline, and all kinds of precise information that most pilots don't really want to know about. Of course, the purpose is to generate the values needed for performance calculations, but it does serve to embarrass novices flying the airplane, with every detail of their transgressions recorded. The upper deck on F-WWDD is laid out with large and comfortable seats that are used when the aircraft goes on demonstration flights. But also hidden in the lower deck are a couple of galley carts laden with wonderful coffee, fresh salads, and baguettes stuffed full of cheese and cold meats—better catering than is usually found on airlines in these frugal times.

Our original plan was to approach Châteauroux airport for practicing some actual landings, from the south and fly a visual left downwind for Runway 22. I spotted the airfield coming into view as a chat with ATC reveals that the wind now favours Runway 04. A quick burst of French between Pascal and Michel is followed by an inquiry as to whether I would agree to a straight-in visual to 04. I must look startled, as Pascal feels bound to explain that this would mean not only saving time but that I could do a 180° turn at the 22 end and take off immediately.

Thus, my first-ever landing on the A380 goes from what was looking like a relaxed visual approach to an ILS-equipped runway to a rushed straight-in without any visual aids whatsoever—not even a VASI (Visual Approach Slope Indicator).

We rapidly 'dirty' up the airplane, extending the gear and flaps early. Unfortunately, I am high for most of the approach and follow Michel's advice of not aggressively recovering the 3° profile, as there is runway to spare and conditions are good. I achieve 'on-slope' at about 500ft AGL (above ground level), and in what seems to be about ten seconds after making the decision, land a little bit long on the displaced threshold of Runway 04. Not the smooth touchdown I had envisaged, but a rather positive arrival.

As briefed, after landing we use reverse thrust and minimal braking. The 3,500m (11,483ft)-long runway is more than sufficient to slow the A380 to taxi speed. Approaching the end of the runway, Michel once again takes me through the procedure for a 180° turn. The turning pan at the end of the runway has been set up by Airbus with marker boards to facilitate this rather tricky manoeuvre. Approaching the area at 5kt, I set 20% thrust on the outer left engine. As the nose gear approaches the edge of the runway (as seen on the taxi camera) and using the signboards for this purpose as a cue, I turn the tiller full right and gently apply some braking with my right foot. The A380 pivots elegantly as planned. Michel calls out the ground speed and I modulate the thrust slightly to maintain 5kt as we turn.

This manoeuvre is almost ridiculously easy. But it is only accomplished after much practice in the simulator, a thorough briefing, in daylight conditions, on a dry runway, and with support from crewmembers who are intimately familiar with it. Chances are that if we have to perform the same manoeuvre for real, it would be at a diversion airport, at the end of a long day, and probably on a wet runway. Let us hope that need will never arise.

Once we are lined up on Runway 22, Pascal runs through the After Landing and Before Takeoff checklists in rapid time, we receive clearance from the tower, and are off again. Roll down the runway, rotate at V_r, and take the A380 up as if I'd been doing this for years. A fairly steep climb after takeoff toward the northeast and we are en-route to Chalon-Champforgeuil, located in the heart of the Champagne region.

The runway at Chalon runs north south (17/35) and is set amongst rolling wheat fields. We need to keep well away from the bustling Paris TMA (Terminal Control Area), but even then it is busy with the TCAS (Traffic Alert & Collision Avoidance System) painting a number of 'bogeys'. However, the good flying weather makes it all quite easy, and I see the airfield from some distance away.

Using the handy FLS (FMS Landing System) approach procedure, we'd set up the FMS to allow a full instrument approach despite the clear conditions. This is an attempt to salvage my pride and have a more stable approach than was possible at Châteauroux. The plan works well. A gentle turn and I am established on final to Runway 35.

This time the approach is rather more leisurely and definitely more stable. Shortly after the A380 crosses the threshold, on speed and on profile, I hear the auto-call intone "Thirty feet." Realising that the speed has crept up a fraction, I pull the thrust levers before the system can command "Retard." A slight increase of pitch attitude as I feel the aircraft being cushioned by ground effect, and just as I think I have overdone it and am about to float, F-WWDD makes a gratifyingly smooth touchdown.

I heave a sigh of relief as Michel and Pascal congratulate me—whether on my luck or skill I dare not ask. Taxiing clear of the runway I bring the aircraft to a full stop. It is now time to swap seats with one of my colleagues and raid the galley for replenishment.

By early in the afternoon we are done for the day, another group of our fellow-trainees will fly the evening session. We all make the obligatory trip to the Airbus souvenir shop so we can load up on T-shirts, stickers, key chains—all emblazoned with 'A380', of course—to ensure our bragging rights when we return home. After a spot of rest at the hotel we meet colleagues at the neighbouring bistro for an aperitif.

There are times, such as this, when I really love my job! ✈

Chapter 4

First operational flight

On August 10, 2008 dawned hot and hazy in Dubai. The brutal summer heat of the Persian Gulf was at its peak. But I leapt out of bed bright and early as this was going to be a landmark day for me. Finally, several months after my training had commenced, I was going to get to fly the Airbus A380 on a scheduled commercial flight.

My first A380 flight on line service would be from Dubai to New York's John F. Kennedy Airport. This was the first destination for the Emirates A380 using the sole aircraft the airline had taken delivery of thus far, registered A6-EDA.

Flight preparation

A modern airplane on a long-distance route such as Dubai to New York requires a complex preparation process. The probable routes, from a variety of options, have to be decided early and appropriate over-flight approvals obtained. In this case, the flight would cross multiple national boundaries and also use the North Atlantic Track System (NATS) en route to JFK. This requires careful planning, as an optimized route must be selected depending on forecast winds and weather conditions. These details are taken care of by a veritable army of flight dispatch officers.

The flight crew first sees what is ahead when a flight plan is produced and uploaded to the system. Most pilots will log into the company information system from home, to get a 'sneak peek' at what lies ahead. That is exactly what I did as soon as I got enough caffeine into my system that morning.

Still in my pyjamas, I logged on to the computer and searched for my flight plan. There it was probably not the final version, but close enough for preparation. The route was a fairly standard one departing Dubai to the north, over Iranian airspace initially, then proceeding over Russia before turning west to cross Poland, the North Sea well north of the UK, over Iceland and Greenland, then Canada and the USA.

Nothing much new there – I had done the route many times before on the Airbus A340, as had the other crew members. That morning there were four of us, which is standard for a long-haul flight. What *was* unusual is that all four of us were captains. The normal crew complement is a captain and a first officer designated as the 'operating crew', and a second pair who would be the 'relief crew'. The rostering system selects the crew based on preferences entered by the individual pilots and its own algorithms. But because this was a brand-new aircraft and everyone needed exposure to 'line operations', there were four captains today.

All four of us were old friends. My 'partner' for today was Mike O'Grady, an Australian who'd flown with me on the Airbus A310 and was a project pilot on the A380 – he knew the aircraft better than any of us. Of the other crew, Suhail Hashim had been in Air Lanka with me, and we had joined Emirates at the same time. The fourth, Hesham Essawy from Egypt, was also an instructor on the aircraft. Four very experienced pilots from a diversity of backgrounds – it was going to be a pleasure to share the flight deck with them.

At the airport

Airport preparations were routine. The flight crew team discussed the proposed flight plan, checked the weather and ensured that all documentation was correct. It was a perfect summer's day in the northern hemisphere. Practically no weather en route – New York was forecasting thunderstorms for later in the afternoon, but we were due to land well before that.

The cabin crew were also ready to go. We had a fully booked flight, and expected some very enthusiastic passengers, all delighted to be among the first to fly in an A380. The cabin crew also anticipated a busy time meeting the expectations of the customers, but their feelings were of optimism and excitement.

In keeping with the enthusiasm, we all made it to the aircraft earlier than usual. 'EDA' was a hive of activity. It had been sitting on ground overnight since arriving from New York. The cabins had been cleaned and replenished, but catering was now going on board. It also seemed that every airport employee with a pass allowing him or her to be there was staring at the interior in awe. The crew had to thread their way through the crowds to reach their stations. As I eased myself into the left seat of the A380, I could see passengers crowding by the windows of the departure lounge and taking 'selfies' with the gigantic airplane as the backdrop.

Pre-flight

Pre-flight preparation on the flight deck is often one of the busier parts of a flight. Setting up a complex aircraft is time-consuming, especially when there are constant interruptions. Knowing that this was going to be the case, Mike and I, the operating crew, settled into our seats and began preparation. Hesham was deputized to assist us by doing some of the tasks that could be accessed from the 'jump seat'. At the door, to deal with all the hundreds of requests and questions that would inevitably surface, we stationed Suhail – all 6ft 6ins of him.

This task-sharing worked well, and we were able to get the aircraft ready in time. As it was a full flight, the aircraft was heavy. Conditions were hot, with the temperature pushing 40°C even this early in the morning. Coupled with the low atmospheric pressure that is typical in the Gulf, we would need the longest runway, 12R, for departure.

Finally the last of the passengers were on, loading of baggage complete, and all the doors were closed. Obtaining start-up clearance was a breeze; no ATC delays for the only A380 at the airport. My flight logbook shows we pushed back at 0909 local time – only a few minutes behind schedule. The ground crew had done an exemplary job in getting the flight out.

Engine start was routine with the big turbines working nicely, and we began our stately journey to the take-off point. One of the relief pilots kept an eye on what was happening in the cabin through closed-circuit cameras which gave us a birds-eye view of the cabin crew working frantically to get everyone seated and both decks prepared for departure. Just as we arrived at the entrance to the runway the 'Cabin Ready' ECAM message was displayed on our screens.

Departure

With checklists complete and showing green on the Electronic Checklist, it was a matter of receiving clearance from the tower and smoothly placing the thrust levers in the TOGA detent. The FADEC applied power, and as I lined the aircraft on the centre of the runway, four pairs of eyes watched as the ECAM confirmed the thrust setting was where it should be.

"Man Flex, SRS, RWY, Auto thrust blue," said Mike as the instruments showed us all was well. The '380' accelerated majestically down the runway. As we approached the midpoint of the runway Mike called "Vee One," signalling that we were now committed to fly, and then "Rotate."

I smoothly moved the sidestick aft, and after a slight pause the nose of the aircraft rose in response. I held it steady and the rumble of the main wheels faded away. "Positive climb," called Mike, and with a glance at my instruments I responded, "Gear up."

That began an amazing chorus of groans and squeals as the massive landing gears retracted into their respective bays. Once that process was over silence reigned, and the aircraft climbed smoothly away. It was a wonderful feeling, as the earth sank back and the huge machine began doing what it was designed to.

The climb-out was routine, with the aircraft behaving exactly as expected. Weather was good, clear, but with some haze closer to the ground. Once we passed through this layer and headed out over the Straits of Hormuz, the view through the big flight deck windows was lovely.

Top of climb was reached uneventfully, and the relief crew left the flight deck to get some rest. We could see through the cameras that the cabin crew were busy with the service, and that the lounge at the rear of the upper deck was already filling up; despite the early hour, premium passengers were determined to start enjoying the luxuries of the A380 at the earliest opportunity.

Cruise

Initial cruise was routine but busy. There were a lot of new 'toys' for us to play with, so we both familiarised ourselves with the aircraft systems as the workload decreased.

We checked and re-checked the route between the printed Operational Flight Plan (OFP), which was programmed in the Flight Management System (FMS), and what the newly programmed LIDO electronic charts were showing. In between routine radio calls to ATC and the many frequency changes, this kept us busy as we headed toward Russian airspace.

We had a few visitors to the flight deck too. Since the 9/11 terrorist attacks in 2001 this had become a rarity, but we had several Airbus technical people on board who had specific permission to enter the cockpit. They too wanted to see their 'baby' in operation, so we spent a fair bit of time asking and fielding technical questions as the automated systems did their thing. An Airbus technical pilot on the flight, Nicholas D'Otreppe, was on the flight deck for much of the time, and he proved to be a valuable resource later on.

The fuel system on the A380, with its 'inverted gull wing', is especially complex. Fuel is shifted between tanks in order to optimize wing loading, and we studied this at some length. It was all settling down to be a nice routine flight to JFK, and we even began discussing what we should do on our layover in the 'Big Apple'.

Beginnings of trouble

The aircraft was behaving impeccably, all systems were normal, weather was fine, and we were making good progress. Moscow was to the northeast of our position as we started to turn toward the west. Due to prevailing winds the flight wasn't following a strict 'Great Circle' routing which would have taken us close to the north of Greenland; rather, we tracked along a 'defined route' passing over Iceland and southern Greenland.

Airports suitable for the A380 were always a challenge. The sheer size of the aircraft required an ICAO Code-F airport for unrestricted operations. These were generally newer airfields and few and far between –

especially in Europe where many airports were originally built in the 1940s and '50s.

This fact was always lurking in the back of our minds, but we didn't expect it to be an issue. Just then one of the cabin crew entered the flight deck to inform us that a passenger had been taken ill. The crew had made a PA announcement for any medical personnel to present themselves and were on the satellite phone to Med link (a 24-hour medical services provider) to analyse the situation. With almost 500 passengers on board, one person feeling unwell was not cause for alarm, so we continued the flight.

That ubiquitous Irishman 'Mr. Murphy' must have been on board that day, though, as the situation did not improve. The crew had two doctors and a nurse assisting them. But because of language difficulties they were unable to fully ascertain what the passenger, a young girl, was suffering from. Both her parents were with her, but couldn't articulate what was wrong with their daughter.

A nightmare scenario was unfolding – eerily similar to another I had faced many years ago on another flight. That has been alluded to in Malcolm Gladwell's book *Outliers: The Story of Success*. But on that occasion I was flying an A340-500, an aircraft type with which I was well familiar. Now, it was my first flight on a brand-new airplane, of which the airline still had only one 'copy'. An emergency diversion was going to be challenging, to say the least.

The difficult decision to divert

There is an old axiom in aviation: "Don't make a decision until you absolutely have to." Rushing to a conclusion can lead to an unhappy outcome; a considered decision is usually a much better one.

We had to gather information. By this time both Hesham and Suhail were back with us – it was 'all hands on deck'. I handed over control and went to take a look at the situation. The cabin was in chaos. The girl's mother was obviously terrified and weeping uncontrollably. The father wasn't of much help either. I was able to spend a few minutes with one of the doctors – his prognosis was grim. The medical team figured that the girl was suffering from toxic shock following recent abdominal surgery, and her body temperature was falling. She was wrapped in a thermal blanket and they were doing everything possible to stabilize her, but it now seemed that a diversion was inevitable.

Rather than getting in the way, I returned to the flight deck and designated Hesham to liaise with the medical team and report progress. If we were going to divert, we needed to make some crucial decisions very soon.

Mike and I had a quick discussion on the flight deck. The aircraft had been close to maximum take-off weight, so we were much heavier than maximum landing weight – dumping fuel overboard was going to be imperative. My heart sank; oil had just hit a historic high of USD 135 a barrel, so this was going to be an expensive operation.

The diversion

Mike got on the satellite phone to Dubai while Suhail and I (we summoned Nicholas back too – no time for crew rest or watching movies) figured out the best place to go. Moscow was not far away but neither of us wanted to divert there – the use of the metric system and other non-standard practices left over from Soviet days made it a hard place to operate to on a good day. Warsaw (Poland) was ahead, but none of us had ever been there and it was not an Emirates destination. Vienna was, but it was notoriously windy and had narrow runways – getting the big beast in there would not be simple. As Nicholas pointed out, we had to dump fuel, and at the maximum rate of 2500 kg/min it would take time to get the weight down. This was a very good point – we did have time to spare, which would help us to manage the workload.

Ultimately there was only one real choice: Munich. Europe's newest airport was Code-F compliant and an Emirates destination with which we were all familiar. It also gave us enough time to jettison a little more fuel. So EDDM it was going to be.

A quick call on the interphone to the cabin confirmed that the patient was still OK, or at least hadn't deteriorated, and that the time we would take to reach Munich should be acceptable.

I looked at the other two pilots and took a deep breath. "OK chaps, let's plan a diversion to Munich with a medical emergency. We need permission to jettison fuel immediately and priority clearance."

"Mike, please let ATC know," I continued. "Suhail, if you could get the current weather and calculate the landing performance for Munich that would be great."

The team went into action as if this was a routine mission. ATC was excellent as always, and we were given a radar heading direct to the initial fix of Runway 26R, which was a comforting 4,000m in length. The weather was excellent, and even at our expected landing weight of 450,000 kg (way in excess of the maximum 'normal' 396,000 kg landing weight) we would have sufficient 'real estate' for a safe landing.

The next item on the agenda was to let people know what was going on. I handed over control to Mike and got on the PA.

I told the passengers what most of them already knew: that we had a very sick little girl on board; and in order to get her to hospital we were going to land in Munich. I also informed them that we would be jettisoning fuel, so they shouldn't be alarmed if they saw fuel streaming out from the wings.

That done, we pulled up the electronic 'Fuel Jettison' checklist and commenced wasting a lot of money. If memory serves we 'dumped' over 50,000 kg that morning, which is about 16,500 US gallons. Fuel cost around USD 3.30 per US gallon at the time, so about USD 55,000 worth of jet fuel went overboard. The most I've ever spent in that short a time.

Little did we know at the time that aviation 'anoraks' using scanners tuned to ATC frequencies were monitoring our 'saga'. They were discussing the situation in real time and debating where we should be diverting to, or even whether we should deviate at all. Taking advantage of the clear weather, a photography enthusiast on the ground using a powerful telephoto lens captured dramatic pictures of 'EDA' with jettisoned fuel streaming like smoke trails in its wake. Someone in the aircraft also took photos of the fuel jettison and, using the on-board Wi-Fi, uploaded the pictures to the Internet. Thankfully, we were unaware of all the 'Monday morning quarterbacks' doing their thing while we concentrated on executing a diversion that could have potentially put our careers on the line.

The dumping of fuel as seen from the ground and posted on the internet

But those thoughts were not in our minds as we calculated and double-checked our performance, got the 'Overweight Landing Checklist' ready, briefed for the approach and continued to monitor the state of our patient. The tension in the flight deck was acute – about the only factor in our favour was the beautiful summer's day with unlimited visibility and no weather to speak of.

Approach and landing

From the top of descent to landing the flight deck had a rather surreal air about it. We worked together to plan and carry out an emergency diversion. All checklists and preparations were complete. We could see Munich Airport in the distance through the haze. None of the usual chatter on the radio and radar vectors for traffic. We were on a discrete frequency, already established on a long final to the runway and cleared to land. The moment of truth was coming close.

I remember staring out the window. The autopilot was still engaged and tracking the ILS perfectly. All I had to do was to disconnect it and land the aircraft – gently. At 450,000 kg this would be the heaviest landing I had ever done. The flying training and familiarisation in Toulouse, which was my only experience in the aircraft, was at less than half this weight.

A stray thought intruded. This was the only A380 Emirates had (as already mentioned). If I were to land it too hard and damage the aircraft, not only would it make the headlines but also signal an end to my career. That was not a pleasant line of thinking, so I pushed it aside and concentrated on the landing.

The smoothness of the touchdown apart, the briefing had emphasised the required runway length. MUC's 4,000-meter runway was more than adequate, but we had to be careful of brake temperatures. As it was summer, the brakes would get hot and take a while to cool down before we could depart again.

Despite so many critical items on my mind the landing was thankfully uneventful. My touchdown was not as smooth as I would have liked, but it was definitely acceptable. We selected maximum reverse thrust in order to spare the brakes and utilised the full length of the runway, exiting at the high-speed taxiway A2 at the end.

Munich Airport had helpfully sent a 'follow-me' car to guide us to the appropriate parking stand. As we turned slowly onto the taxiway and followed the vehicle, I ensured that the reversers were cancelled and called for the 'After Landing Checklist' – with a huge sigh of relief.

Touching down at 60,000 kg above Maximum Landing Weight

On ground

As we taxied to the remote stand that had been prepared for us, one of the pilots pointed out a medivac helicopter landing ahead of us. An ambulance was waiting, and as soon as the aircraft was secured the emergency medical teams rushed on board. The patient was whisked into the ambulance and taken across the ramp to the helicopter. We watched it fly away, and made a quiet prayer wishing that little girl well.

After completing the checklist and technical logbook, I went back into the cabin to thank the medical team that had been assisting us. I then had to shake the hand of what seemed like every passenger on the airplane! They were all cheerful and supportive – no one seemed to mind that their journey had been interrupted so abruptly.

We still had a lot of work to do, and half the flight to complete. But for the moment it felt good to stand up and have a cup of tea. A glass of champagne would have been much nicer, but not, unfortunately, feasible under the circumstances.

At this stage the enormity of what we had done was slowly sinking in. It was great to be part of a close-knit team and a company with *esprit de corps*. The 'can do' culture of Emirates began to kick in. A friendly face suddenly appeared in the flight deck – it was the Emirates Station Manager in Munich, Kurt Maier-Längsfeld.

On this Sunday at the height of summer Kurt was enjoying his weekend, but had heard of the diversion and didn't hesitate to drive in. Seeing his familiar face was a relief. It got even better – Reggie Thompson, an old motorcycle buddy of mine from Dubai and a Licensed Maintenance Engineer to boot, had been on an Emirates cargo flight that day in Munich. Seeing the A380 landing he had finished his work on the freighter and hurried over. Reggie was familiar with the Emirates way of handling aircraft, so we had a team on ground too.

Then another smiling face appeared – this time it was Thomas Torsten-Meyer, VP Operations of MUC Airport, who came to the aircraft to offer assistance. Thomas very kindly waived all landing and handling charges, and even authorised free fuel! His only request was a couple of photographs and a look at the aircraft. He was not the only person who wanted to see what the Germans called the 'uber plane'. Every passenger bus that was delivering people to aircraft at other stands seemed to drive by for a chance to see the A380 up close. We felt like rock stars!

The transit was slowly coming together. A flight plan was rushed over from the airport – Dubai Operations had obtained all the clearances and an arrival slot at JFK – albeit a few hours late. The fuel was going on board, and Reggie was working with the LTU airline technicians to ensure they handled the A380 correctly. But then we ran into a problem.

Overweight landing

The aircraft had landed approximately 60,000 kg above the certified maximum landing weight. A critical check needed to be conducted before we could legally depart. I was quite sure my landing was well within limits, but without verification we could not dispatch.

This was a problem, and we had to find a solution. Or else we'd be here overnight. In all the planning that had taken place, the need for an overweight landing analysis at a diversion airport had been somehow overlooked. The only way to gather the data was to 'burn' a CD on the maintenance computer located on the observer's seat. But first it was necessary to obtain a blank CD as one is not carried on board the aircraft. If we didn't have a CD, then the data could not have been collected and the flight wouldn't depart.

Thankfully, the EK (Emirates) Station Manager was able to obtain a blank CD from a personal contact at the airport. The LTU ground engineer (Stefan) and Reggie were able to access the maintenance PC and write a data set exceeding 400 MB to the CD. Maintenance Control Centre (MCC) in Dubai required a 600 KB data file to be extracted from this and emailed to them.

On ground in Munich – Suhail, Reggie, Mike and the author

Again, no provision had been made to accomplish this task. We were forced to use my personal laptop and extracted the files to a USB flash drive – strictly non-standard but the clock was ticking. Reggie then transported this USB drive to the passenger terminal and emailed it to MCC using a computer in the EK lounge. The analysis was subsequently completed and the verdict was issued: my touchdown had been smooth enough such that no warning thresholds had been triggered. An ACARS message was sent to the aircraft authorising continuation of the flight without a heavy landing maintenance inspection.

We finally departed MUC/EDDM approximately 2½ hours after landing. Brake cooling had been the least of our troubles, and it was a relief to be airborne again.

Munich to New York

Mike was the Pilot Flying on the next leg, and we fell into the routine of a normal trans-Atlantic flight. After top of climb somewhere over the North Sea, Mike and I handed over the controls to Suhail and Hesham, and took the opportunity to use the crew rest facilities. I must have been tired, as I fell asleep as soon as I got into the bunk, waking only when someone shook me to say we were approaching JFK.

The descent into New York was routine. No special treatment as at Munich, and ATC subjected us to the usual vectoring and delays on a busy Sunday evening. But the weather over Cape Cod was perfect, and I could see Nantucket Island and Martha's Vineyard quite clearly as we were vectored around New York's busy airspace.

As luck would have it, those thunderstorms had made it to New York before we did, and the duty runways were 22L & 22R. We requested 22R – at 12,079 ft (3,680 m) it was long enough for the A380, even though the runway was reported as being damp following recent rain. Runway

22L is 8,400 feet long – plenty for the A380, but we weren't feeling particularly adventurous. We'd had enough excitement for one day. The airplane was well below maximum landing weight and the weather was fine. It looked like a normal approach and landing, albeit on a runway much narrower than the one in Munich.

But the aviation gods must have sensed my optimism and decided to do something about it. New York ATC has a reputation for being quite demanding and almost rude. So when the controller asked us, politely, "Emirates 201 we have a request" during the initial part of the approach, alarm bells started sounding.

As Mike was the pilot flying, I replied, "Emirates 201, go ahead."

"Emirates, are you able to vacate Runway 22R at the intersection with Runway 31L?" was the response.

Mike and I looked at each other in alarm – that was only about two-thirds of the normal length; this was going to be tricky. Just about the same length as 22L that we'd decided to *avoid*.

"Emirates 201 – we will calculate the numbers, but what is the reason?"

"Well, there is a disabled aircraft on Taxiway KB, and we need you to stop before that, otherwise spacing might be an issue."

Oh no! – more complications. Luckily, the other two pilots were still on the flight deck, and they worked out that it was possible to stop in the available length – just. More hard deceleration and heated brakes were in our future.

Mike and I were both tense as we got closer and began to see the runway. Just as our eyes confirmed it, the controller said, "Emirates 201, disregard. Full runway length available – you are cleared to land Runway 22R." The gods must have decided to give us a break – and we had certainly earned it.

Mike made a nice, smooth touchdown, and we used the full length of the runway to exit right at the end. As we slowly taxied to the terminal, all four of us exchanged high fives – it had been a long day and a memorable first flight – but at last we were at our destination. Eighteen hours after leaving Dubai the flight was finally over.

The crew and passengers remained cheerful and happy as we disembarked. In spite of everything we encountered we'd coped with the situation well and hadn't broken our one and only precious A380. We were all looking forward to a couple of days of well-earned rest in Frank Sinatra's 'City That Never Sleeps'. ✈

Postscript: *Sadly, the next day we heard the news that our young passenger, whose illness had precipitated the diversion, had not survived. She had made it to hospital, but the doctors were unable to save her. It was a sad end to what had been a long and exhausting episode for all concerned.*

Emirates Airbus A330, A310 and A380 at Munich that day

Chapter 5

A380 in Service-One Year and Counting

This was originally published in Airways *magazine, January 2010. In two previous issues of* Airways *the author described the Airbus A380 training program: in the classroom, simulator, and 'hands-on' flying. Now, with the first year of line flights in his logbook, he discusses the techniques, requisites, and his experiences and opinions of flying the 'big bus in the real world'.)*

'Fat Boy'—one of the controllers has nicknamed us. As in, "standby pushback clearance; Fat Boy is passing behind you and he's very slow."

Looking at the Airbus A380 from the side it is easy to see why the name is appropriate. The 72.7m (238.5ft) length appears foreshortened because of the 24m (78.7ft) height. It looks rather like a bologna sausage with a vertical bit stuck on. Elegant it is not.

Gibes aside, it is usually a relief to be moving. Probably the most trying part of flying the big Airbus is the pre-flight preparation phase. Airbus's philosophy of the 'less paper cockpit' has been taken to great lengths. Most of the preparation is electronic and paperless, but it is still complicated and time-consuming. One of the first tasks the pilots accomplish when they sit down is to retrieve the flight plan from the ACARS (Aircraft Communication Addressing & Reporting System) and update the OIS (Onboard Information System). This lets the aircraft 'know' the departure and destination airports, plus the route.

Next in sequence is the independent calculation of the preliminary take-off performance. This is accomplished using the TOPA (Take-off Performance Application) on the OIT (Onboard Information Terminal). The sheer bulk of the A380 is belied by its performance, which is very good for most airports. Nevertheless, it is important to have a long enough runway; 4,000m (13,000ft) is ideal as it means there are no limitations. At sea level the A380-800 is capable of lifting its maximum payload almost all the time. The edge of the envelope appears only as temperatures approach 40°C (104°F). Until then, lifting max payload allows us to carry 203t (447,500 lb) of fuel for the MGTOW (maximum gross take-off weight) of 569t (1,254,6501b). This in turn comfortably allows over 15 hours' endurance, enough for most city pairs, making the A380 a true long-range airplane. Most days, though, the aircraft tends to 'volume out' before reaching the MZFW (maximum zero fuel weight) of 366t (807,0001b). With a full aircraft, a ZFW of about 362t (798,0001b) seems to be typical.

In addition to the usual initialization of flight deck systems and configuration of switches, the A380 requires pilots to make extensive use of the OIS and NSS (Network Server System). A 21st century aircraft, the A380 is fully networked. The NSS has two sides: Avionics and FLT OPS (flight operations). This is controlled by a two-position switch on the side consoles, which select either system for display on the OIT, the screen that the pilots look at.

The NSS Avionics and the airplane's avionics systems communicate in both directions via the SCI (Secure Communications Interface), which is mainly an engineering function. However, only one-way communication is permitted from the NSS Avionics side to the FLT OPS side. The latter, which has such niceties as TOPA and LDA (Landing Distance Application), is equipped with its own server, router, printer, a wireless LAN (local area network)—this works only on the ground and we cannot surf the 'Net—and three laptop computers that hold most of the aforementioned applications, plus operations manuals, electronic flight folder, and navigation charts. This equipment truly makes the A380 the 'electric jet', and my teenage sons would probably be quite comfortable operating all of it. In fact they would probably set it up to run by itself via SMS while they do something more interesting-like Tweeting with their friends.

Also used early in the pre-flight set-up phase are the TOPA, FCOM (Flight Crew Operating Manual), and LSA (Load Sheet Application). Crucial to this process is determining the specific gravity of the fuel, as this is needed to calculate the load and CG (centre of gravity) position. The A380 can carry up to 323,546l (84,122USg) of Jet A-1, the actual weight of which depends on atmospheric conditions such as ambient temperature.

Final ZFW is received on the flight deck as an email via the NSS, to which the pilots respond with the final fuel figures. The load sheet is then sent as another email with an accompanying hard copy on the cockpit printer. All this exchange of emails makes you realise why Airbus thoughtfully provided a full-size keyboard for each pilot.

Also contained in the OIS is a full suite of the Jeppesen (or LIDO) charts, all electronically displayed on the NCA (Navigation Charts Application). Full-colour, re-sizable charts can be displayed for both pilots, in either day or night mode. The ability to enlarge key portions of the charts is especially useful for captains, whose eyesight is being slowly eroded by Father Time. It is also possible to enter the full route of flight into the NCA, which then shows the appropriate chart in full colour and even pans it as the flight progresses. The days of having to continually fetch new charts to remain orientated are now history.

Finally, when all the 400-plus punters are onboard, it is time to close the doors. The pilots tend to keep a close eye on the passenger load, particularly in the premium cabins.

Sadly, the aircraft has made its debut during the worst recession the world economy has known for a long time. Carrying a lot of cargo—a huge revenue-generator in hard times—is not possible if the aircraft is full of passengers. Therefore, high-revenue customers are the key to operating profitably. Because the bean counters tend to keep information such as breakeven load factors very private (particularly in this hyper-competitive environment), crews try to estimate the success of the aircraft by using their own techniques. Some clever pilot, who had the patience to crunch the numbers, has concluded that if the premium cabins are full, the aircraft will at least break even. Anything more than this is a profitable run, so a busy economy class and full premium cabins are welcome sights. Thus, the passenger load is scrutinized closely to reassure us that the flagship is a going concern. Without exception, we all love flying the big machine and want to keep it in the air making money.

Pushback and engine start

Pushback is a stately affair, and moving the massive weight of a fully loaded A380 takes a special tug. Start-up is routine, with engines started in pairs. The ones on the right wing, no's 3 & 4, are brought to life first, to provide hydraulic power for the body landing gear steering. Once the two on the left wing (no's 1 & 2) are fired up, we release the engineer and perform the flight control check. A quick read of the electronic checklist to make sure nothing is left out, and it is time to start moving.

Taxiing provides the first real challenge. This is a large aircraft with a lot of inertia, and it needs room. In an ideal world we would only operate to ICAO (International Civil Aviation Organization) Code F airports with nice wide taxiways (see sidebar). Manoeuvring the big 'bus on narrower taxiways is a challenge. Extensive use of the taxi cameras is necessary to ensure that the airplane stays within the taxiways, without any embarrassing re-arrangement of taxiway edge lights. The key is to keep moving: any speed less than 5kt and the A380 tends to lose momentum. Conversely, turning at anything more than 9kt leads to groans of protest from the nose wheels, which 'scrub' at these speeds. Even a little moisture on the surface exacerbates the situation; that's when we really move around like a galleon in the doldrums.

The airplane's 80m (262.5ft) wingspan also creates a problem when there is another large aircraft on a parallel taxiway. Caution is the order of the day, as we make slow but steady progress to the duty runway.

At MGTOW on a humid, tropical day, the A380 will have a V_1 (take-off safety speed) of around 170kt with a 'Flex' or assumed temperature thrust setting in the high to mid-forties Celsius. So, plenty of thrust is available if needed. It is only as the OAT (outside air temperature) approaches 40°C that full thrust or TOGA (take-off go around) becomes necessary.

Departure

Taking off is both a non-event and a relief. The Rolls-Royce Trent 900 turbofans spool up easily with hardly a sound. Acceleration is smooth and uneventful, V_r (rotation speed) approaches rapidly, and the aircraft practically springs into the air with plenty of runway ahead. It's almost as if the A380 senses it is entering its true environment, as only gentle pressure on the side-stick is sufficient to get us gracefully airborne. Raising the landing gear is the first major event after take-off and is accompanied by an astonishing chorus of groans and squeals as all 22 wheels drag themselves into the gear bays. Once this noisy interlude is concluded, the A380 continues to climb in silence.

Initial climb is uncomplicated and brisk. At MGTOW the aircraft usually climbs initially to the low-thirties (thousands of feet). Flight level 320 (32,000ft) is a fairly typical altitude to begin with, and the cruise speed there is usually Mach 0.85 (the Mach number being the ratio of the airplane's speed to the speed of sound, the latter speed varying with air density which decreases as altitude increases). This is brisk enough to silence the boys flying 'light twins' (such as the Boeing 777) that also cruise at this speed; smaller Airbus types cruise at Mach 0.83 or less, a source of much amusement to Boeing drivers.

Climb-out in a crowded TMA (terminal control area) can be quite an ego trip. We are a source of considerable chatter among other pilots; some of them even badger ATC (air traffic control) with an occasional request for a radar vector to facilitate air-to-air photos. Of course, we ignore all this clamour and serenely continue to our cruise altitude, impervious to the envying glances of lesser aircraft types.

Top of climb and cruise

Top of climb (TOC) leads to a flurry of activity as we scan the systems and the OIS. The pilot-flying (PIC) usually brings up the IFPA (In-Flight Performance Application) to calculate the optimum cruise levels, and check on engine parameters in cruise and drift-down altitudes. IFPA can be used in the climb as well, but is typically referred to at TOC. It contains a wealth of information that used to be buried deep in the manuals, but is now available digitally at the pilots' fingertips. No more peering at a faded or torn monochrome page in a manual—simply input the actual parameters (altitude, temperature, wind, weight) and look at the exact performance data needed. Magic!

The pilot-not-flying (PNF) is typically responsible for ensuring that the electronic charts reflect the actual route of flight. It is possible to build the entire route and have it displayed in real time for each pilot with the relevant airways highlighted for easy recognition. The application can also be used to call up ATC frequencies and the wealth of information found on the printed charts. But because it is displayed on demand, the display is free of all the clutter seen on the paper version. The actual process of building the route is not automated and can take a few minutes. Most of the time it is not completed during the pre-flight phase because of time constraints, but left until the workload drops off.

Cruise is generally a relaxed and easy phase of flight. The cockpit windows are huge (much bigger than on other Airbus types) and afford a great view. As for the flight deck itself, this is spacious enough to allow the pilots to stand up occasionally and have a good stretch. Of course, the slide-out table is wonderfully handy, and a novelty for pilots who have transferred from the 'other maker's' airplanes, where there is a control wheel and yoke in the way for the entire flight.

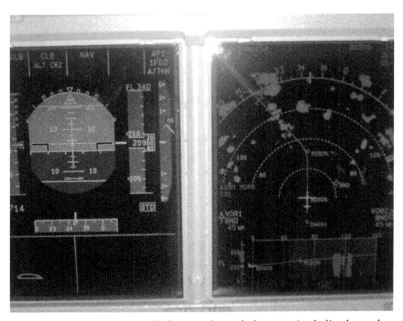

The weather radar is particularly good, and the vertical display—located on the lower half of the ND (navigation display– see above)—makes avoiding storms quite simple. The 'crosshatch' display of weather, whereby the system decides if any weather is below the airplane, is very accurate. Initially, most pilots experimented with the system by taking it out of the automatic mode and varying the tilt and gain to satisfy ourselves that it worked as advertised.

Eventually we overcome our scepticism and learn to trust the system except on the stormiest of dark nights. The ND has range selection of 10-320nm making it possible to see the next waypoint on all but the longest of legs.

The CPDLC (Controller Pilot Data Link Connection), which allows us to text-message with ATC rather than communicate over sometimes-scratchy voice connections, is very well integrated with the cockpit displays. Using the cursor and keyboard located near the MFD (Multi-Function Display) the pilots can generate all the routine messages that need to be sent to ATC and, in free-text mode, anything else.

During a long-haul flight the A380 burns about 13t (28,650lb) of fuel an hour. While this sounds a lot, fuel consumption per seat-mile is astonishingly good. The caveat is that there is not much of a difference between a full and empty aircraft. DOW (dry operating weight with no passengers, baggage, or fuel, but full catering, water, oil, and hydraulic fluid) is around 303t (661,500lb), so the payload is not much more than 60t (132,000lb)—20% of the DOW on the best of days. To carry this load over a long stage will burn roughly 125t (275,600lb) of kerosene. If the aircraft were totally empty of passengers and freight, we would still expend more than 90t (19,500lb) of fuel to fly the same route. So, passenger loads are crucial to profitability, which is why we keep such a close eye on the numbers.

Depending on the cost index currently in use, the aircraft tends to cruise anywhere between Mach 0.8.1 and 0.86. The higher end of the envelope is especially useful as it allows us to make up any slight delays on ground and ensure our valued customers reach their destination on time. Turbulence cruise is surprisingly fast too, with the aircraft rarely having to slow down much below Mach 0.83 no matter bad the weather. The A380 rides the bumps very smoothly, much better than some earlier models from the same stable.

The A380 is very popular with passengers, its capacious cabin, especially on the lower deck where the ceiling is almost 3m (9.8ft) high, belying the fact that we are travelling in a metal and plastic tube some 6mi (10km) above the surface of the planet. Also contributing to the pleasant ambience are the very quiet interior and relatively low cabin altitude.

The lounge at the rear of the upper-deck – picture credit Pintrest

Descent and Approach

Both descent and approach phases are also usually routine. ATC controllers tend to make us reduce speed early to accommodate slower types and get the sequencing right. Approach speeds are refreshingly slow. Even at MLW (maximum landing weight) of 391t (862,000lb) the A380 has a V_{ref} of 141kt and needs less than 2,000m (6,550ft) of runway to land, even when the surface is wet. To put this into perspective, in the event that a primary runway (such as 34L in Sydney or 16 in Melbourne) is not available for some reason, be it weather or operational, the A380 can quite comfortably land on the shorter crosswind runway.

The final stages of descent come quickly, the A380 tending to be a bit 'slippery' on the glideslope. Because the airplane is very aerodynamic it is easy to become a little fast in the initial stages of the approach. This is solved, however, with extension of the A380's mighty landing gear being sufficient to provide the requisite retardation.

Final approach is very stable with not much thrust required to maintain speed. At 140kt (or less, most of the time) observers on ground comment how the A380 tends to float across the threshold. This is difficult to appreciate from the cockpit as we are now working quite hard to ensure the arrival is as smooth as the rest of the flight.

Landing and parking

Crossing the threshold at 50ft, power is gradually reduced, and the PF applies gentle backpressure on the sidestick. The trick is to keep the attitude steady rather than try to flare as in earlier types. Because of the cockpit height, there is a slight illusion. Just when it feels that the A380 is going to float and embarrass us in front of all the other aircraft waiting for take-off, the aft wheels touch down with a gentle sigh—and we have arrived. It is difficult to make a firm landing with the A380, although this writer has achieved that feat on more than the odd occasion.

The airplane is programmed to lower the nose as part of the 'flare law', but a slow release of pressure is a good idea. Thrust reversers are available immediately and the autobrake kicks in quickly and smoothly, making a high-speed intersection, such as A2 off Sydney's Runway 34L, not a problem even on a wet day. As with all examples of Airbus airplanes of this generation, the auto-thrust system automatically disconnects on landing.

'Fat Boy' makes good use of the 'instinctive disconnect' buttons on the thrust levers (obviously redundant at this stage as the system has disconnected automatically). After landing, these buttons can be used to disconnect the autobrake system, making for a smooth reversion to manual braking. A fitting end to a perfect touchdown.

As we enter the taxiway, the most important task is to slow down. Being much lighter than we were to start with, taxi speeds are not that much of an issue. If anything the aircraft tends to get away from us, and because the brakes are fairly warm by now it is important to keep a close watch on developments. When faced with a long taxi to the stand, many pilots tend to shut down the inboard engines once the cool-down time (approximately three minutes at idle) has passed. The outboard engines are very high off the ground, so foreign object ingestion is unlikely, even though at most airports the engine nacelles hang over the grass. By taxiing in on two engines, brake wear is greatly reduced and fuel is saved as well. Our final turn to the parking stand is also rather majestic. The last thing the crew wants after a long flight is to stop too far or, even worse, too close to the gate.

Summary of performance

Pioneers always tend to get a lot of press, good and bad. On balance, the A380 has had a very good introduction to service. Some initial teething problems were solved quickly. As the aircraft has matured and utilization increased we have obtained a better idea of what it takes to operate the beast. Spares are always going to be an issue. Given that there are so many onboard computers, keeping a large stock of spares is a financial burden. After some time in service, the airline now has a feel for what needs to be kept ready for frequent use. Other than the system control units (computers), of which there are hundreds, one problematic issue is the fuel system. 'Fat Boy' carries an enormous quantity of fuel and this is stored in no less than 11 tanks: five in each wing (outer, mid, inner plus two feed tanks) plus the tank in the THS (Trimmable Horizontal Stabilizer). There are 20 fuel pumps in the tanks alone.

One of the reasons for this complicated system is the dramatic curvature of the gull wing. This feature imposes a disadvantage compared to airplanes with flatter wing profiles that enable an easier flow of fuel to the engines with far fewer tanks and pumps. In the A380 the number of tanks and pumps is probably—and partially—to counteract the effect of fuel 'pooling' at the wing root, although this is a pilot's opinion and engineers who designed the aircraft might disagree. Whatever the reason, the inescapable fact is that this contributes to a complex system that demands considerable time spent transferring fuel between tanks.

Obviously much of this activity is dictated by fuel burn and the need to keep the feed tanks full. Airbus's trademark CG control—which maintains the airplane's CG slightly forward of the aft limit, thereby optimizing cruise performance—also transfers fuel to the trim tank early in the flight and then incrementally forward in the course of the cruise. In addition, the load alleviation transfer serves to reduce structural loads on the wing by transferring fuel to the outer tanks as required.

However, with 20 pumps constantly shunting fuel around to optimize CG position and wing loading, there is a lot that can go wrong. Particularly vexing is the failure of an outer tank pump. Unless a spare is available, this throws out the normal fuel distribution. It then becomes necessary to uplift the required fuel and manually shift it before engine start, in order to arrive at the correct loading for abnormal operation. A time-consuming process that cannot be accomplished until all the fuel is onboard, this inevitably leads to a long delay. Indeed, there are more than a few pilots in the company who wish they could carry a spare fuel pump in their luggage, just in case.

Further developmental changes to the A380 and its growth potential should focus on weight savings. One of the first factors to be addressed must be the reduction of the aircraft's DOW by at least 10t (22,000lb) to counter the weight limitations mentioned earlier. This will permit an additional 16t (35,000lbs) of fuel to be carried at a typical operational ZFW of 360t (794,000lbs).

Accordingly, if structural modifications will allow the MGTOW to be increased beyond its current limit of 569t, an 18-plus hour endurance would be possible (available thrust not being a limiting factor). This would bring routes such as Singapore-Los Angeles (7,600nm/1-1,000km) or even Singapore-New York (8,300nm/ 15,500km) within range of the aircraft. Thus, the ability to carry 500 passengers nonstop between any two city-pairs would make the A380 a genuine world-beater.

If it hasn't become obvious by now, this writer is a 'Fat Boy enthusiast'. The A380 is certainly a great airplane in more than just the visually obvious sense; it is the best Airbus I have had the privilege of flying, and handles beautifully; flawlessly in fact. If the A380 seems complicated to operate, it is worth noting that this is only the first iteration of a family that is likely to see out the careers of an entire generation of pilots. When the Boeing 747 was introduced 40 years ago, it must have been much more complicated to operate, even with a flight engineer on hand. Significantly, the workload on the A380 is only high during pre-flight preparation. At all other times it is a perfectly relaxed and simple machine for the pilot and—in case I have not made my point often enough already—a joy to fly.

Another serendipitous pleasure for the still relatively small number of A380 pilots worldwide is that with only a handful of the type in operation thus far, our privileged group is akin to an intimate and exclusive club. There is a greater-than-usual sense of camaraderie within the fleet, seeing familiar faces regularly as part of a small team—a happy close-knit group of people who are doing what they love, playing with a big new toy. ✈

With hindsight, the writer was too sanguine on the aircraft's future. As we shall see in the following op-eds, the aircraft became the victim of high fuel prices and the fracturing of the 'hub & spoke' model it had been designed for.

Chapter 6

Who killed the Airbus A380?

(This first appeared as a column in the Daily FT *of Sri Lanka in June 2019.)*

As American author Mark Twain remarked in 1897, "The report of my death was an exaggeration."

The Airbus A380, flagship of the world's largest airliner manufacturer and culmination of an estimated USD 16 billion development program, is alive and well. Currently flying with 14 of the world's most prestigious airlines, with Japan's All Nippon Airways (ANA) having just taken delivery of its first A380, the giant aircraft is still being produced.

But sadly, A380 production is due to be halted by 2021 when the last aircraft will be delivered to its biggest customer, Emirates. Between now and that date, production will be slowed to about one airframe a month, barely enough to keep the assembly line ticking over.

What happened?

When Airbus began developing the concept of a massive airliner, dubbed the 'A3XX' project, the world was a different place. At the time the project was launched, in 1999, jet fuel, which accounts for between 15 to 30% of an airline's expenses, was priced at a generational low. The airline business was booming and Boeing, undisputed leader in the airliner game, was easily profitable, with its venerable 747, appropriately dubbed 'Queen of the Skies', a huge profit-generator for the Seattle,

59

Washington-based manufacturer. Airbus was the upstart trying to find a niche for itself while battling the US giants. Determined to have a complete 'suite' of airliners, Airbus management decided to launch a rival to the 747.

Boeing was sceptical. Their forecasts showed a totally different market projection and they were not keen on updating the 747. Finally they did so reluctantly, launching the 747-800, but were more focused on creating the 787 Dreamliner – a twin-engine mid-size airliner designed for a more fragmented market.

Emirates Airline, then an upstart too, was an enthusiastic customer for the Airbus A380, being the first to announce an order in April 2000. Air France, Singapore Airlines, Qantas and Virgin Atlantic would follow the same year, showing initial enthusiasm for the type.

Emirates A380 pre-delivery in Hamburg – picture credit Airbus

Lufthansa and Qatar Airways joined the 'A380 club' shortly thereafter, Federal Express ordered the freighter version, and Emirates tripled its A380 order. Airbus was delighted; the flagship was going to fly.

Tellingly though, the major aircraft leasing companies, who are the primary buyers of new airliner types, were very cautious in placing orders for the A380. It was obvious that the market was more sceptical than Airbus.

More complicated than they thought

Flight testing and then producing an aircraft of this complexity proved to be much harder than even Airbus had imagined. Innumerable delays dogged the program, and the A380 missed many delivery milestones. The complex nature of the airliner market means that excessive delays allow the customer to cancel orders with few penalties. As Airbus missed many projections on the delivery timeline, customers began having second thoughts about the viability of the giant, double-deck aircraft.

The aftermath of the World Trade Centre attacks in September 2001 dented the confidence of many airlines, just as the A3XX project was launched and oil prices began climbing too.

The US-led invasion of Iraq sent oil prices to a new all-time high. The market reached a peak of almost USD 150 a barrel of oil in 2007, concurrent with the A380 approaching 'entry into service'. The global financial crisis of 2008 further dented customer confidence, and cancellations started pouring in.

Entry into Service

The Airbus A380 was triumphantly and flawlessly launched into service by Singapore Airlines in October 2007, becoming an instant customer favourite. (*picture below – credit SIA*) Airbus's 'super salesman' John Leahy confidently forecast demand for over 1,300 aircraft in the 'very large' category which included the B747-800 and the Airbus A380.

But the writing was already on the wall. Jet fuel was at an all-time high, the A380 that could weigh up to 570,000 kg when fully loaded with passengers, cargo and

61

fuel, would burn over 13,000 kg of fuel every hour. An empty A380 with no fuel, passengers or cargo on board, still weighed in excess of 300,000 kg.

By contrast, archrival Boeing's 787 Dreamliner had a maximum weight (full of passengers and freight) of around 239,000 kg, with its two engines burning about 5,000 kg an hour. The contrast was obvious – in a high fuel price world, the Airbus 'whale' was just too heavy and thirsty.

Only one lover

Emirates and Qantas introduced the A380 in 2008, with Lufthansa and Air France following soon after. The Airbus sales team worked frantically to gather orders for the 'whale'. For a while it seemed that they were succeeding. Many of the world's flag-carriers placed small orders (see box), but only one was a 'true believer'.

Emirates Airline, led by the forceful and visionary Tim Clark (now Sir Tim), was determined to build a 'mega hub' in Dubai. The A380 suited his vision perfectly, bringing in almost 500 passengers per airplane into Dubai, where they would change to another and reach their destination on all six continents that Emirates' network encompassed.

By configuring the aircraft with luxurious First and Business Class cabins, plus a 'cocktails lounge' on the upper deck and economy class on the main deck, Emirates had effectively two separate areas. Dubai airport was built in such a way that the premium passengers could board the aircraft directly, without having to mingle with those in 'steerage'.
Emirates uses 162 of the 235 A380s delivered worldwide – a ratio that is totally unprecedented in the industry.

Airline	Orders	Deliveries
Air France	10	10
All Nippon Airways	3	1
Asiana Airlines	6	6
British Airways	12	12
China Southern	5	5
Emirates	*162*	*109*
Etihad Airways	10	10
Korean Air	10	10

Lufthansa	14	14
Malaysia Airlines	6	6
Qantas	12	12
Qatar Airways	10	10
Singapore Airlines	24	24
Thai Airways	6	6

A niche markets

Several airlines that originally ordered the aircraft have cancelled it completely. A few went out of business during the economic slowdown as well. The only lessor with an order, International Finance Lease Corporation (ILFC), cancelled it completely in 2011.

As the numbers above show, the A380 has, at best, a niche market. Even the most efficient airlines, with large home markets generating huge passenger numbers, can only seemingly maintain around a dozen A380s. The only exceptions to this are Singapore Airlines, a 'super-connector' itself, and Emirates.

However, the fact that Singapore Airlines has returned three of the original A380s delivered to the lessor, who has been unable to place these aircraft with other customers, says volumes.

Emirates re-thinks the A380

Even Emirates, the only large user of the aircraft with over half the existing hulls, has now been forced to rethink its commitment. With Airbus and the major engine manufacturers declining to design a newer and more fuel-efficient A380, Emirates has been compelled to order the smaller A350 model instead.

In a recent (pre-COVID-19 crisis) statement Sir Tim Clark has mentioned that Emirates plans to retire its fleet of A380s by the mid-2030s.

What is the future of the A380?

No airline will be able to order the A380 from the factory anymore. But numerous units will still be available in the secondary market.

Emirates will, of course, remain a user of the aircraft for the foreseeable future, with at least 15 more years of service envisaged. Most of the flag-carriers such as Lufthansa, Air France and Korean Air will probably continue to use their limited fleets to service capacity-constrained city pairs. Singapore Airlines too will continue operating the aircraft for the same reason. Willie Walsh, CEO of International Airlines Group (IAG), which owns British Airways and Iberia, has gone on record that he may acquire pre-owned A380s, if the "price point is feasible".

One possible new user could be Turkish Airlines, by some measures the largest airline outside the USA, who has just moved to a brand-new airport outside Istanbul that can accommodate the giant airplanes. The older Atatürk Airport was too small for the A380.

An exercise in hubris

The A380 has proved to be an expensive learning experience for Airbus Industry. It has now established itself as a major player, holding a market share equal to that of its archrival Boeing. Between them, the two manufacturers have an effective duopoly of the market.

Boeing's future forecasts have turned out to be more accurate than those of Airbus, with the 787 proving to be the modern aircraft of choice for airlines, as demonstrated by 1,400 orders against 890 for the A350. The list price of the 787 is significantly less than its Airbus rival, but production is sold out for many years. This will probably allow Airbus to claw back some share of the market.

Boeing, meanwhile, is facing a hugely expensive debacle with the 737 MAX programs, which is a topic for another day.

How Airbus will account for the huge development cost of the A380 (estimated at over USD 16 billion) remains to be seen. It is obvious that the 290 firm orders will barely pay the costs of producing the aircraft, with the research and development expense having to be absorbed by profits on other aircraft types in the stable.

While the A380 will continue to delight passengers for a long while, it will also probably be the last 'mega project' that takes to the skies. The jetliner has changed the world in ways no one could foresee just a few decades ago. It is sad to think that we will not see anything this ambitious launched again. ✈

Chapter 7

The demise of the 'Uber Plane'

This appeared as a column in the Daily FT in May 2020)

n June 2019 this column asked **<u>"Who killed the A380?"</u>**. By then it was bvious that Airbus's flagship was not a sales success, and its eventual lemise was only a matter of time. This writer predicted that the aircraft vould probably fly on for 'at least 15 years'.

As Warren Buffett famously said, 'Forecasts tell us more of the orecaster than of the future.' True in this case; my intimacy with, and ffection for, the A380 obviously coloured my judgement. Then again, vho could foresee what destruction a microorganism could cause to our ociety and economic system?

Why would an airline choose the A380?

A380 operators worldwide fall into several categories. The major buyers of the aircraft are the world's 'super connectors' such as Emirates and ingapore Airlines, with their huge hub airports. Some aspirants to this ousiness model such as Qatar Airways, Etihad Airways and Korean Air lave also acquired the giant aircraft.

lirlines with congested home airports, for example British Airways, Qantas, Air France and Lufthansa, had a convincing business case for the A380. The third category comprises what would be called 'wannabes': lirlines without a persuasive need for the capacity but didn't want to be eft out of the 'club'.

Airline	Entry	Total	Engine Type
Air France	2009	10	Engine Alliance
All Nippon Airways	2019	2	Rolls-Royce
Asiana Airlines	2014	6	Rolls-Royce
British Airways	2013	12	Rolls-Royce
China Southern Airlines	2011	5	Rolls-Royce
Emirates	2008	115	RR/Engine Alliance
Etihad Airways	2014	10	Engine Alliance
Korean Air	2011	10	Engine Alliance
Lufthansa	2010	14	Rolls-Royce
Malaysia Airlines	2012	6	Rolls-Royce
Qantas	2008	12	Rolls-Royce
Qatar Airways	2014	10	Engine Alliance
Singapore Airlines	2007	24	Rolls-Royce
Thai Airways	2012	6	Rolls-Royce

Source: Airbus Orders & Deliveries data, as of 31 December 2019.

The fallout from the pandemic

COVID-19 has changed the world and probably killed off the giant airplane too. At the time of writing there isn't a single A380 flying anywhere. A solitary aircraft, belonging to China Southern, recently completed a number of flights, but that appears to have been the only one in use.

Air France, the fourth airline to introduce the A380, has confirmed that it will permanently retire its entire fleet of ten aircraft. Lufthansa (14 A380s) and British Airways (12) have placed most of their examples of the type in long-term storage. Lufthansa has permanently retired six of its A380s, along with five Boeing 747s and seven Airbus A340s. In fact, the demise of *all* four-engine airliner types seems inevitable.

Etihad and Qatar have grounded their A380 fleets and do not appear likely to operate the type anytime soon.

Both Singapore Airlines and Qantas, early users of the double-deck 'superjumbo', have undertaken large-scale refurbishing of the interiors of their older A380s. In such instances, a bill of over USD 20 million per

aircraft would not be excessive. Whether this will compel them to keep operating those aircraft post-COVID remains to be seen, but for now those fleets are grounded too.
(*below SIA aircraft at Alice Springs, Australia. Credit – The Australian*)

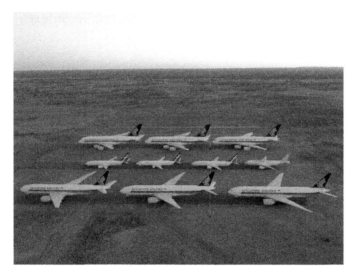

Emirates are the outlier

The Gulf giant, Emirates, is going to be the hardest-hit A380 operator. Dubai's congested airport was the reason why Emirates' huge fleet of A380s worked so well pre-COVID. The giant machines would fly in from the farthest
parts of the world with four connecting 'waves' of arrivals and departures allowing multiple daily flights to many major cities. In the context of mass-tourism Emirates showed that the A380 filled an undeniable niche.

With its luxurious premium cabins garnering a loyal following in more affluent markets, plus a huge network of economy passengers from less wealthy customer segments filling the 'lower deck', the two-tier product was a perfect fit.

Post-COVID it is hard to say when this sort of traffic will resume. The economic concerns apart, the patchwork nature of travel restrictions may make it very hard to fill the 500-odd seats in an A380 on a daily basis. Emirates' entire A380 fleet is currently grounded in Dubai and the airline's President Sir Tim Clark has flatly stated, "...the A380 is dead" in a recent interview. But he has also gone on record claiming that the airline expects to operate the aircraft again.

Other recent reports indicate that Emirates wants to cancel the eight A380s being assembled in Toulouse. The penalty for this is rumoured to be USD 70 million *each*–putting other cancellations in context.

Stored Emirates aircraft at Dubai – picture credit Emirates

What is the cost of a permanent grounding?

The actual delivery cost of an individual aircraft is a closely guarded secret. However, it is safe to say that most A380s cost considerably in excess of USD 250 million each in 2019 dollars, with some of the smaller operators probably paying close to USD 300 million per airplane.

Most airlines have the aircraft on an operating lease, meaning it is a fixed-term contract with the asset owned by the lessor; or a finance lease, whereby a financial institution funds the purchase of the aircraft.

The world's four major leasing companies (AerCap, Air Lease Corporation, Avolon and GECAS) do not own any A380s–they had no confidence in the aircraft. This has proved to be a wise decision.

Smaller lessors who own significant numbers of earlier deliveries are likely to take a substantial capital hit as the aircraft are retired. With no secondary market (only a single pre-owned A380 has been successfully placed) and a limited need for spare parts, even the salvage value of the giant is greatly diminished.

Generally speaking, aircraft engines carry a value as much as the airframe when new or freshly overhauled. But used A380 powerplants, particularly of Engine Alliance manufacture, have almost no demand. Even the Rolls-Royce Trent 900 has little value as other versions of this engine (the Trent 700 on the Airbus A330; and 800 on the Boeing 777) are also reaching the end of their life cycles.

It is likely that owners of the world's A380 fleets will have to bear a very expensive write-down of their assets, which in a world on the brink of a Depression, is a sobering thought. ✈

Chapter 8

Roger Béteille– the man who reinvented the commercial airliner

(This was first published in the Daily FT *August 2019)*

The visionary engineer, pilot and manager who led Airbus to some its most significant decisions, passed away in June 2019.

Béteille, who was the head of French aircraft manufacturer Sud Aviation's flight-testing section, was made technical director of the infant Airbus consortium when it was formed in 1970. He was largely responsible for making English the working language of Airbus and for recognizing that the products of the new company must be acceptable to the huge North American market. He drove that program when he was made General Manager of Airbus in 1975.

The size of the fuselage of the first Airbus airliner, designated the A300, was influenced by Béteille, who saw the need for accommodating freight as well as passenger baggage in such a large aircraft. To allow for optimum cargo space, the underbelly hold was designed to hold two LD3 containers back-to-back. The resulting cross-section of 222 inches became the defining size of successive generations of Airbus aircraft, including the A330 & A340 series flown by Sri Lankan Airlines.

The sale of 23 A300 aircraft to Eastern Airlines, at the time the dominant airline on the USA's east coast, marked a turning point in the fortunes of the European challenge to US hegemony in building airliners. Since that first landmark sale, largely the work of Béteille's team, hundreds of Airbus machines have been sold to airlines in North America.

Roger Béteille - the father of Airbus. Picture credit Airbus Industrie

The key move in the game, however, was Béteille's decision to build a radical new smaller aircraft and compete in the 'narrow-body' market, then dominated by the Boeing 737 and McDonnell Douglas DC-9. In designing the Airbus 320, the Europeans decided to maximize the use of new technology. This included not only the pioneering 'fly-by-wire' digital flight control systems (which supplanted the traditional steel cables and pulleys that aircraft used at the time) but also electronically-driven system monitoring, checklists and failure analysis, known as ECAM (Electronic Centralized Aircraft Monitor).

Béteille's right-hand man was the test pilot and engineer Bernard Ziegler – another Airbus legend. They worked in close concert to ensure that many innovations were incorporated into the DNA of the Airbus aircraft; such as the fly-by-wire system and the 'envelope protections' about which Ziegler's evangelical zeal convinced his boss to incorporate them.

The digital revolution that was unleashed by the A320 completely rewrote the way that aircraft were designed and how pilots flew them, with large control wheels being replaced by small side-sticks and a table in front of each pilot. Part of this dramatic change was driven by a need to differentiate the Airbus 320 from the existing competition. By replacing many of the paper checklists and handbooks that were then the norm, Airbus changed not only the entire airline industry but also how pilots interacted with the aircraft.

So successful did the A320 concept become, subsequent Airbus models followed the same path, allowing seamless transition for pilots between smaller and larger aircraft in the same 'stable' or 'family' of types. This led to huge savings for the airlines. Boeing was forced to follow suit with digital systems for the 777 wide-body family which was launched a few years later. As we have seen, Boeing's decision to not build a 'digital' narrow-body aircraft as well, has cost them dearly in the recent past.

By the time Béteille retired as its President in 1985, Airbus was established as a genuine player in the high-stakes aircraft manufacturing space. He was described as the 'father of Airbus', and the A350 final assembly building was named after him in 2012. (*picture below*)

Roger Béteille passed away peacefully at the age of 97 on June 14, 2019, with his beloved company firmly established as the world's dominant aircraft manufacturer. A legacy the great visionary would be very proud of. ✈

About the author

Suren Ratwatte is a pilot and lifelong aviation enthusiast. He flew with Airlanka and Emirates for over 30 years, logging just under 20,000 hours in a variety of aircraft types, including the Airbus A380, Boeing 777 and Lockheed L-1011.

After leaving Emirates in 2015 he served as CEO of SriLankan Airlines before retiring in 2018. He currently lives in Melbourne, Australia and writes extensively on aviation topics including vintage airliners.

You can follow him on Medium, Twitter (@SurenRatwatte) and on his website surenratwatte.com

Printed in Dunstable, United Kingdom